An Encyclopedia of
MYTHS AND
LEGENDS

HAYDN MIDDLETON

INTRODUCTION

The Greeks, Romans and Celts lived in Europe in ancient times. They all had their own beliefs and ideas, and their own gods and heroes. Stories about gods and goddesses are usually called 'myths', while stories about heroes and heroines are usually called 'legends'. The Greeks, the Romans and the Celts had exciting myths and legends.

Some of the Greek and Roman gods and heroes were quite similar. This is because the Romans conquered the Greeks, and introduced many Greek figures into their own mythology. The Romans later conquered Britain, where the Celts lived, so some of the same figures crop up again in the Celtic tales.

Sometimes a word within an entry is printed in *italics*. This means the word has its own entry elsewhere in the encyclopedia, which you can look up to find out more about it.

In this encyclopedia, the first word of each entry is printed in **bold** type. These words are called headwords, and they tell you what the entry is about.

Pronunciation guides are shown for some of the headwords. The stressed syllable in the headword is printed in **bold**.

Each headword is followed by an icon, which tells you, at a glance, if an entry is about something Greek [**G**], Roman [ℝ] or Celtic [ℂ].

GUINEVERE [**gwen**-a-veer] ℂ: King *Arthur's* beautiful queen, who fell in love with Sir *Lancelot*, a Knight of the Round Table. Although she was a mortal, she was also a kind of goddess of Britain.

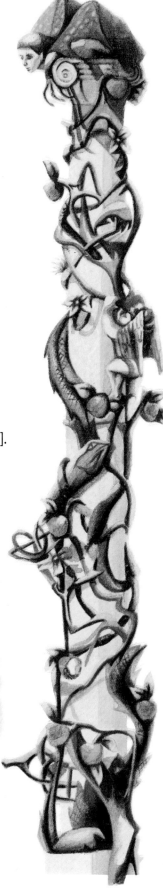

ACHILLES [a-**kill**-ees] **G**: warrior son of a *Shapeshifter* sea-goddess, who dipped him in the River Styx (see *Otherworlds*) as a baby to make him invulnerable. However she held him by his heel, which the waters did not touch. When he went to fight in the *Trojan War* an arrow hit him in the heel and killed him.

AENEAS [ay-**nee**-ass] **R**: prince of Troy, who escaped, with some relatives and followers, after the *Trojan War* and sailed to Italy. There he settled, married the daughter of a local king, and later became king himself. He is seen as the legendary ancestor of the Roman people.

APOLLO G: young god of music, archery, prophecy, healing and the care of animals. *Homer* usually called him 'Phoebus Apollo' (bright Apollo) and he often took the form of a sun god.

ARTHUR C: great Celtic king who ruled over Britain after it stopped being part of the Roman Empire. Tales about Arthur come from many different countries – including Wales, Scotland, France, Germany and England – and in most of them Arthur is a heroic war-leader and wise ruler. Some Welsh poets described how ferocious he could be; they called him 'Red Ravager' because for seven years neither grass nor plants would spring up wherever he walked. Arthur's followers were the Knights of the Round Table. The ultimate challenge for a Knight of the Round Table was to find the *Holy Grail*. One of the knights – Mordred, Arthur's nephew – badly wounded the king at the battle of Camlann. Arthur did not die but was taken to the island of Avalon (see *Otherworlds*) to be healed, so that one day he might return.

ATHENE G (Minerva ℝ, Sulis ℂ): goddess of wisdom and war, she also protected cities. Instead of being born, she sprang – already dressed in armour – from the head of *Zeus*. According to myth, Zeus had a raging headache and asked his son to relieve his agony. His son took an axe and split open Zeus' head, releasing Athene.

BACCHUS [back-us] ℝ (Dionysus **G**): god of festivities and wine – which some say was his invention. Bacchus' mother died before his birth, but Mercury (see *Hermes*) saved him and sewed him into the thigh of his father Jupiter (see *Zeus*) from where he was later born. Bacchus was so disliked by Jupiter's wife, the goddess Juno, that she drove him mad. Afterwards he wandered around the world with his wild band of followers.

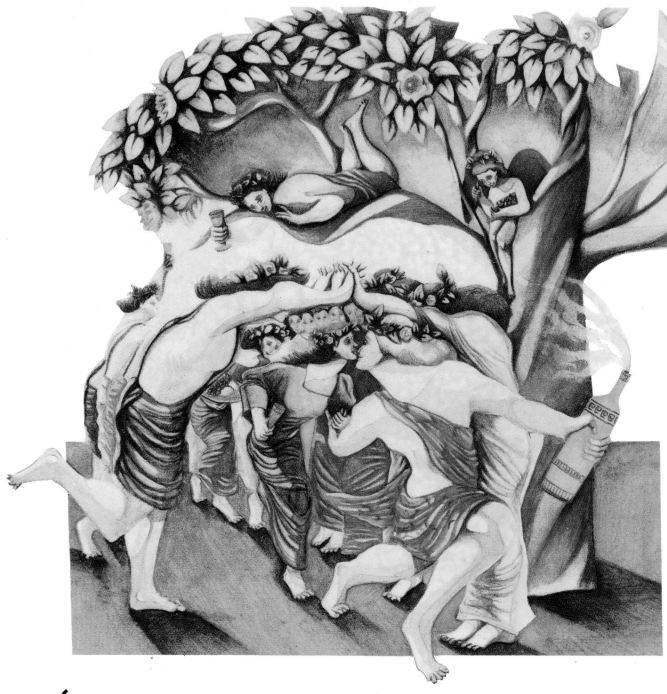

BRAN THE BLESSED C: giant king who ruled over ancient Britain during its *Golden Age*. His sister Branwen married the king of Ireland, and when she was mistreated there, Bran waded across the Irish Sea from his court in Wales to seek vengeance. In the terrible war that followed, almost everyone was killed. Bran's severed head – still alive and able to talk – was brought back home. It was buried inside the White Mount in London, facing France. Legend has it that as long as it remains there, no invaders will ever conquer Britain.

BRUTUS C: Trojan great-grandson of *Aeneas*, who came to a northern island called Albion with other survivors from the *Trojan War*. Brutus drove out the race of giants who already lived in Albion and became its king. The land was then re-named 'Britain' after him.

CAMELOT C: court of King *Arthur*. Carlisle, Somerset, South Wales and Winchester have all been thought possible sites of Arthur's Castle.

CUCHULAINN [koo-hullin] C: greatest Irish war-hero. Usually small and dark, his looks changed hugely in battle. 'The hero's light rose from his forehead,' says a twelfth century story. 'As high, as thick, as strong, as powerful and as long as the mast of a great ship was the straight beam of dark blood which rose from the very top of his head and became a dark magical mist.'

CUPID [kyoo-pid] ℝ (Eros 𝒢): god of love. He was a winged child with a magical bow, and whoever he hit with one of his arrows fell in love. He himself fell in love with the mortal girl Psyche (which means 'breath' or 'spirit'), who finally became immortal too, so that she could be with him.

DAGDA 𝒞: protective craftsman-god of ancient Ireland. He dressed like a peasant and dragged a great magic club behind him on wheels. With one end he killed his enemies; with the other end he could heal those he had slain.

DEIRDRE ℂ: most beautiful girl in Ireland. Before her birth, it was prophesied that she would bring great sorrow. A king had her brought up to be his wife, but she fell in love with another man and ran away with him to Scotland. On returning to Ireland, her lover was killed, then Deirdre killed herself too.

DEMETER [de-**mee**-ta] **G** (Ceres ℝ): ancient goddess of corn, farming and fertility. She and her daughter *Persephone* were known as the 'Twin Goddesses', who nourished all living things. Interestingly, the dead were sometimes called 'Demeter's people' because Demeter was the goddess of the Earth: the resting place of the dead.

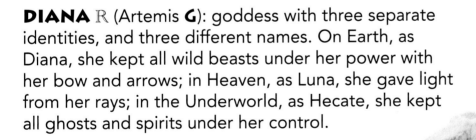

DIANA ℝ (Artemis **G**): goddess with three separate identities, and three different names. On Earth, as Diana, she kept all wild beasts under her power with her bow and arrows; in Heaven, as Luna, she gave light from her rays; in the Underworld, as Hecate, she kept all ghosts and spirits under her control.

EXCALIBUR ℂ: *Arthur's* enchanted sword. Arthur received the sword early in his reign from the mysterious Lady of the Lake who told him that the scabbard was worth a thousand swords and that wearing it would protect him from any wound. When he was taken to Avalon, one of his knights threw it back into the lake from whence it came.

FANTASTIC CREATURES

The Greeks, Romans and Celts lived close to the world of nature; animals and birds played an important part in their lives. The myths and legends of these ancient peoples sometimes featured creatures that were part-human and part-animal – like **Centaurs** and **Harpies**, the **Minotaur** and the **Medusa**. Their stories also had fabulous beasts in them like **Dragons**, which did not really exist, although many people believed that they did. Then there were creatures like the **Salmon of knowledge**, which looked like ordinary fish, but had superhuman powers.

CENTAURS: monsters from Greek and Roman myths which were half-man, half-horse. Sometimes savage and wild, they also had great wisdom. The wisest of all, Cheiron, was the teacher of heroes like *Jason* and *Achilles*.

DRAGONS: in Celtic legend, one of the 'Three Great Plagues of Britain' was the dreadful din made by two fighting dragons – one red, one white. The problem was solved when Lludd, a brave and ingenious king of Britain, lured them with a potion that sent them to sleep, then buried them deep in the ground in highest Wales. But during the troubled reign of King *Vortigern*, they rose again and continued their fight.

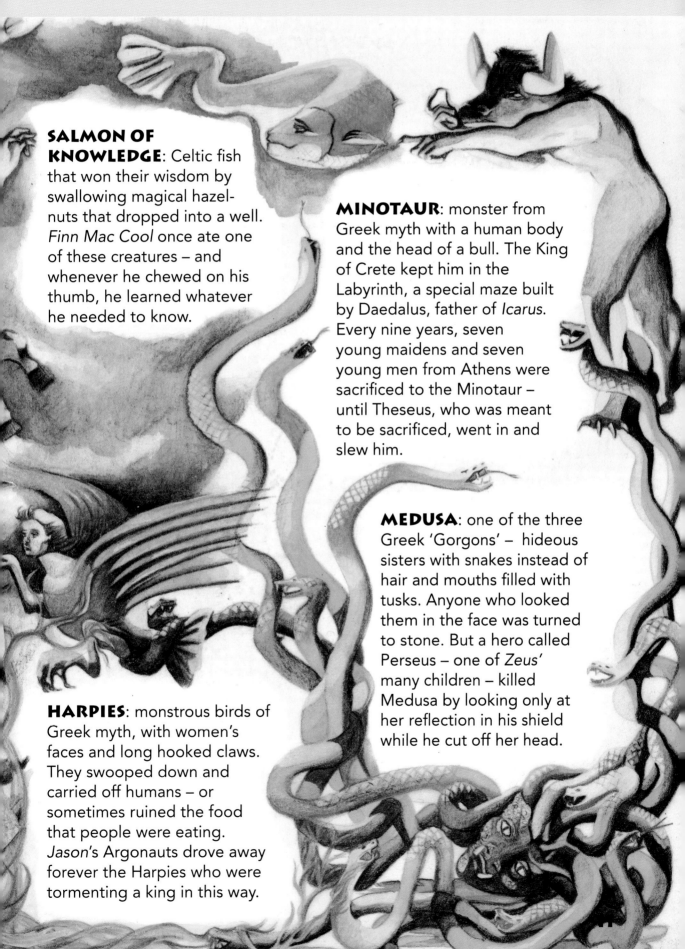

SALMON OF KNOWLEDGE: Celtic fish that won their wisdom by swallowing magical hazel-nuts that dropped into a well. *Finn Mac Cool* once ate one of these creatures – and whenever he chewed on his thumb, he learned whatever he needed to know.

MINOTAUR: monster from Greek myth with a human body and the head of a bull. The King of Crete kept him in the Labyrinth, a special maze built by Daedalus, father of *Icarus*. Every nine years, seven young maidens and seven young men from Athens were sacrificed to the Minotaur – until Theseus, who was meant to be sacrificed, went in and slew him.

MEDUSA: one of the three Greek 'Gorgons' – hideous sisters with snakes instead of hair and mouths filled with tusks. Anyone who looked them in the face was turned to stone. But a hero called Perseus – one of *Zeus'* many children – killed Medusa by looking only at her reflection in his shield while he cut off her head.

HARPIES: monstrous birds of Greek myth, with women's faces and long hooked claws. They swooped down and carried off humans – or sometimes ruined the food that people were eating. *Jason's* Argonauts drove away forever the Harpies who were tormenting a king in this way.

FINN MAC COOL C: Irish warrior-hero, whose war-band was called the 'Fianna'. One story says that, like *Arthur*, he is not dead but sleeps in a cave. Another story says he built the Giant's Causeway in County Antrim.

GOLDEN AGE G R C: past time when life was good and people lived in harmony. For the Greeks and Romans this time was the reign of Cronos (*Saturn* R), for the Celts it was the reign of *Bran the Blessed*.

GUINEVERE [**gwen**-a-veer] C: King *Arthur's* beautiful queen, who fell in love with Sir *Lancelot*, a Knight of the Round Table. Although she was a mortal, she was also a kind of goddess of Britain.

HELEN OF TROY G: most beautiful woman in the world, whom every Greek prince wanted to marry. She finally married one of them, but was kidnapped by a prince of Troy. All her former suitors then sailed to Troy to try to rescue her. So began the *Trojan War*.

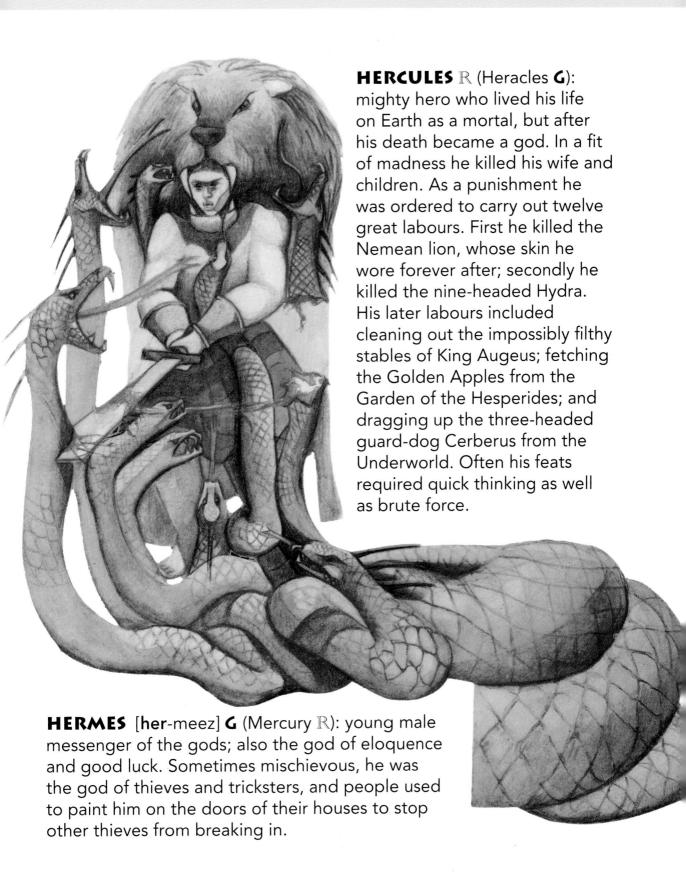

HERCULES ℝ (Heracles **G**): mighty hero who lived his life on Earth as a mortal, but after his death became a god. In a fit of madness he killed his wife and children. As a punishment he was ordered to carry out twelve great labours. First he killed the Nemean lion, whose skin he wore forever after; secondly he killed the nine-headed Hydra. His later labours included cleaning out the impossibly filthy stables of King Augeus; fetching the Golden Apples from the Garden of the Hesperides; and dragging up the three-headed guard-dog Cerberus from the Underworld. Often his feats required quick thinking as well as brute force.

HERMES [her-meez] **G** (Mercury ℝ): young male messenger of the gods; also the god of eloquence and good luck. Sometimes mischievous, he was the god of thieves and tricksters, and people used to paint him on the doors of their houses to stop other thieves from breaking in.

ho-ic

HOLY GRAIL C: mysterious, wonder-working object which appeared in many forms – a dish, a cup, a kind of cauldron and even a stone. Its powers were vast, but few knights were worthy even to glimpse it.

HOMER G: name given to the author of two very long poems about ancient gods and heroes: the 'Iliad', about the *Trojan War*; and the 'Odyssey', about the adventures of *Odysseus* after the War. No one knows anything for certain about this poet – he may even have been more than one person.

ICARUS [i-ka-rus] **G**: son of Daedalus, who invented the Labyrinth on the island of Crete in which the Minotaur was kept (see *Fantastic Creatures*). After Theseus of Athens killed the Minotaur, Daedalus and Icarus helped him to escape. The King of Crete imprisoned them in the Labyrinth to punish them. Daedalus made two pairs of wings from feathers, cord and wax so that he and his son could fly free. Icarus flew too near to the sun, which melted the wax. His wings disintegrated and he plunged to his death.

JANUS R: god who was present in every door, gate and passageway. Usually shown with two faces, one looking back and one forward, to show his knowledge of things past and of things still to come.

JASON G: hero sent to bring back a magical Golden Fleece from the distant land of Colchis. Many other heroes joined Jason in his long and exciting quest; they were called the 'Argonauts' after the name of the ship they travelled in, the 'Argo'. But Jason's greatest helper in achieving his aim was the witch Medea, whom he married. When Jason later deserted her, Medea killed their two children in revenge. Jason then committed suicide, or – in another version of the story – died when part of the rotting 'Argo' fell on him.

JUNO ℝ (Hera **G**): wife of Jupiter (See *Zeus*), and the goddess of marriage and childbirth. She argued bitterly with her husband, who was often unfaithful to her, and she severely punished his lovers and their children.

LANCELOT ℂ: champion knight of *Arthur*, who became the lover of *Guinevere*. When Arthur found out about their affair, the queen was sentenced to death by burning, but Lancelot saved her and briefly fought a war against Arthur.

LARES AND PENATES R: household gods who watched over Roman families. Sometimes these gods were the souls of dead members of the family. Lares also protected streets, highways and whole cities.

LEGENDS OF ORIGIN: tales by which the Greeks, Romans and Celts explained their own earliest history (see *Aeneas* and *Brutus* for origin legends of the Romans and the British Celts). Origin legends often featured a distant *Golden Age*, when life was gentler and happier (see *Saturn*).

LOST LANDS G C: mysterious lands that have been 'lost'. Many old tales are set in places that we can still visit, but some happen in these lost lands. Greek mythology tells of a kingdom west of Europe called Atlantis, ruled over by Atlas (see *Titans*), which sank without trace in a flood. The Celts' Lowland Hundred, a region on the Welsh coast, also disappeared beneath the waves – but even now the bells of its vanished churches are said to ring underwater.

MABINOGION C: collection of Celtic myths and legends, first gathered around the year 1400. The old tales – previously passed on by word of mouth – were written down in Welsh by different authors, and feature *Bran the Blessed*, *Macsen Wledig*, *Arthur* and many other heroes and heroines.

MACSEN WLEDIG [maxen u-ledig] C: Welsh name for 'Roman Emperor Maxen'; hero of a strange tale in the *Mabinogion*. After dreaming of a westward journey, at the end of which a beautiful woman waits, he made the journey and married the woman. This is thought to be a story-version of the conquest of Britain by the Romans.

MAGIC CAULDRONS C: cooking vessels – often from the Otherworld – which had special powers, e.g. the cauldron of the Chief of Annwn (see *Otherworlds*) would not boil the food of a coward; the Irish god Goibniu brewed beer in his cauldron for a feast which made the guests immortal; *Bran the Blessed's* cauldron brought the dead back to life, although afterwards they could not speak.

MARS R (Ares **G**): god of war, who watched over men in battle. To the warlike Romans, he was second in importance only to his father Jupiter (see *Zeus*). Mars was the father of *Romulus and Remus*, the founders of Rome.

MERLIN C: wizard, prophet and wild man who watched over Britain. The Welsh poets say Britain's earliest name was 'Merlin's Precinct'. He served as protector to the boy *Arthur*, and brought him forward to be made king when the kingdom needed him. He remained Arthur's magician and adviser during his reign, but later he went mad and lived wild in the forests.

MITHRAS ℝ **G**: god of the sun. His great deed was the sacrifice of a white bull, which led to the beginning of the world.

NARCISSUS [na-si-sis] **G**: handsome young man, of whom it was said he would live to a ripe old age, provided that he never came to know himself. But when he saw his own reflection in a spring, he fell in love with it. Since he could not kiss or embrace the reflection, he pined away and died of grief.

ODYSSEUS [o-**di**-see-us] **G** (Ulysses ℝ): hero of *Homer's* long poem, the 'Odyssey'. King of Ithaca, and happily married to Penelope, he sailed reluctantly to fight in the *Trojan War*, which he helped the Greeks to win with his bravery and quick thinking. On the return voyage, he made an enemy of the sea-god *Poseidon* after blinding his son, Polyphemus the Cyclops. Poseidon punished him by confronting him with dangers, such as the song of the Sirens which lured men to their death. After ten years Odysseus returned to his palace – to find a hundred and twenty other men competing to marry Penelope, as everyone thought that by now Odysseus must be dead. With the help of his son, Odysseus won back his wife in a great battle – and so brought his adventures to an end.

OEDIPUS [ee-dip-us] **G**: son of the king and queen of Thebes. The king threw him out at birth, because it was prophesied that he would be destroyed by his own son. But Oedipus – saved by a shepherd – survived, grew up and unwittingly killed his father. Then, after defeating the monstrous *Sphinx*, he was made king and married his mother – again, without knowing who she was. When he learned the truth, he blinded himself and wandered into exile.

ORPHEUS G: greatest poet and musician of all time; some say he was the ancestor of *Homer*. He sang so beautifully that even wild beasts were entranced, and rivers stopped flowing to listen. After his death, his head lived on, still singing.

OTHERWORLDS

The Greeks, Romans and Celts had many different ideas about what happened to people after they died. The Greeks told stories about a gloomy underworld kingdom of the dead called **Hades**; this was also the name of its ruler (Pluto ℝ). Not all such otherworld regions were unhappy places: according to *Homer*, the **Plain of Elysium** 'at the world's end' was a kind of paradise. The Celts looked westward to a similar sunset world; in Britain it was called the Isle of **Avalon**, while to the Irish its regions had names like 'The Plain of Two Mists' and 'The Land of the Living'. Sometimes Celtic heroes visited these places even before they died – for example, *Arthur* tried to raid the Welsh otherworld of **Annwn**.

ANNWN [a-**noon**]: mysterious Celtic otherworld that was described as being sometimes underground, or as an island, and sometimes as a 'Fortress of Glass'. *Arthur* led a disastrous expedition to Annwn in an attempt to seize a *magic cauldron*. Three ships full of warriors accompanied him, but only seven men returned – empty-handed.

AVALON: peaceful Celtic island of apple trees. *Arthur* was taken here after he was wounded at the Battle of Camlann. Some people believe that Avalon is really Glastonbury in Somerset, where medieval monks claimed they found the bones of Arthur and *Guinevere*.

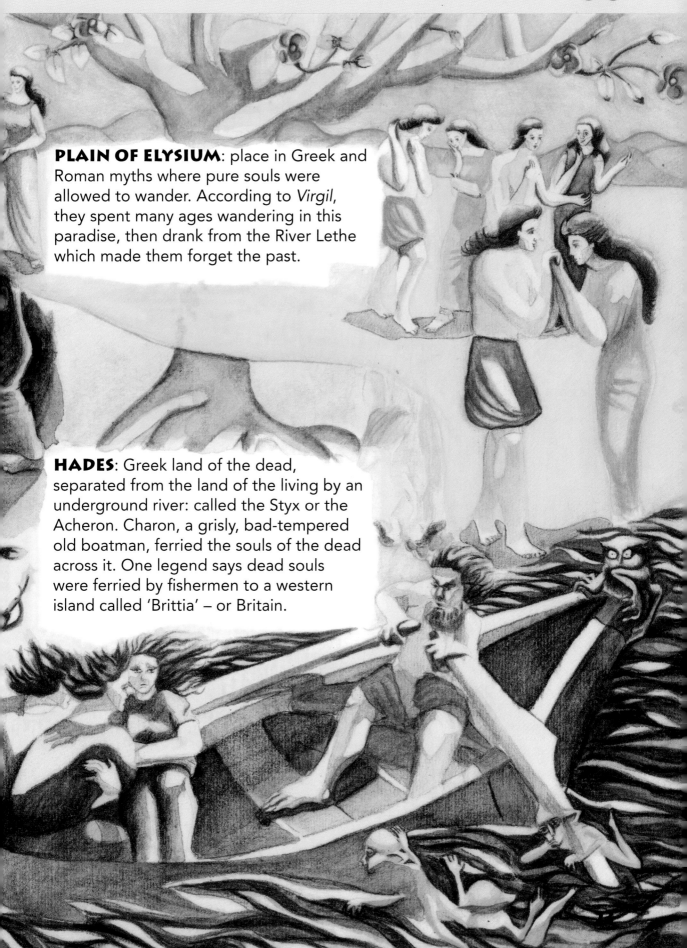

PLAIN OF ELYSIUM: place in Greek and Roman myths where pure souls were allowed to wander. According to *Virgil*, they spent many ages wandering in this paradise, then drank from the River Lethe which made them forget the past.

HADES: Greek land of the dead, separated from the land of the living by an underground river: called the Styx or the Acheron. Charon, a grisly, bad-tempered old boatman, ferried the souls of the dead across it. One legend says dead souls were ferried by fishermen to a western island called 'Brittia' – or Britain.

PANDORA G: first mortal woman, made by the gods and sent to Earth with a box or jar that she was told never to open. Curious about its contents, she disobeyed and out flew Disease, War, Famine and all the other evils and vices which would trouble the world forever after – only Hope remained in the box to help people.

PANTHEON [pan-thee-on] G R C: collective name for all the gods of a people. Some peoples' gods – like those of the Greeks – were closely linked, and often related to one another. The twelve main Greek gods and goddesses lived together on Mount Olympus. They were: *Zeus* (Jupiter R) and his wife Hera (*Juno* R), *Poseidon* (Neptune R), *Demeter*, *Apollo* and *Athene* (Minerva R); Artemis (*Diana* R), Ares (*Mars* R), Aphrodite (*Venus* R) and *Hermes* (Mercury R), Hephaestus (god of craftsmen) and Hestia (goddess of the hearth). The Romans also had other gods like *Mithras* in their pantheon. The Celtic peoples, scattered over many countries, had a more widespread pantheon, e.g. *Bran the Blessed* in Wales and *Dagda* in Ireland.

PERSEPHONE [pur-**se**-fa-nee] **G**: daughter of *Demeter*, who was snatched away by Hades to be queen of his dark otherworld kingdom. Demeter was so grief-stricken that *Zeus* ordered Hades (see *Otherworlds*) to send Persephone back to earth for the summer of each year.

POSEIDON G (Neptune ℝ): fearsome god of the sea and brother of *Zeus*. Like the sea itself, he was changeable and dangerous.

PROMETHEUS
[pro-**mee**-thee-us] **G**: *Titan* who created humankind from clay and brought it to life with the help of *Athene*. When *Zeus* refused to let humans have fire to cook with, Prometheus stole fire from heaven and took it to earth. In revenge, Zeus sent *Pandora* to cause havoc among humankind, and he had Prometheus chained to a rocky peak in the Caucasus mountains. Each day an eagle tore out his liver and each night the liver grew again. Finally *Hercules* shot the eagle and released Prometheus from his age-long agony.

ROMULUS AND REMUS R: twin sons of the god *Mars*, who grew up to be the founders of Rome. Thrown out to die at birth, they were swept along by the River Tiber to a place where the city of Rome would one day stand. A wolf kept them alive, and after many years they returned to lay the great city's foundations. It is thought that Romulus later killed Remus and ruled over Rome until he died, when he became a god.

SATURN R (Cronos G): *Titan* who overthrew his father *Uranus*, then ruled over the *Golden Age* of the world. Although this was a time of peace and plenty for everyone, Saturn was a cruel tyrant. He feared that a child of his own would destroy him, so he ate each of his children at birth. But when the youngest son Jupiter (*Zeus*) was born, his mother Rhea hid him in Crete and gave Saturn a wrapped-up stone to eat instead. Years later, Rhea made Saturn vomit up the children inside him, and they joined with the fully-grown Jupiter to fight a mighty war against the *Titans*. After ten years the new gods were victorious and ruled the world. Saturn was banished to a far-off western isle where he slept in chains, not quite dead yet not truly alive.

SHAPESHIFTERS G R C: gods or heroes who took on the appearance of other creatures – particularly animals or birds. The Roman poet Ovid is famous for writing a collection of poems called 'Metamorphoses'. These poems describe the transformations of Greek and Roman gods and people – often because passion or desire had changed them out of all recognition.

SPHINX G: monster with a woman's head, a lion's body, a snake's tail and an eagle's wings. It menaced the countryside around Thebes by asking passers-by a riddle: 'What walks on four legs in the morning, two legs in the afternoon, and three in the evening?', devouring anyone who could not give the right answer. Finally *Oedipus* replied: 'Man – who crawls on all fours as a baby, then learns to walk upright, and hobbles with a stick in old age.' Defeated, the furious Sphinx flew away for ever.

TITANS G: first race of divine children produced by the Sky (called *Uranus*) and the Earth (known as Ge). Sometimes known as 'the gods before the gods', they included Oceanus, Hyperion, Rhea, Tethys and – last of all – Cronos (*Saturn*). Cronos' son *Zeus* imprisoned the male Titans in Tartarus, which was so far underground that a falling anvil took nine days to reach it. Only the mighty Atlas was spared – but he had to stand for ever at the Earth's edge, holding up the sky on his shoulders.

TRISTAN C: Scottish hero, sent to Ireland to fetch Isolde, the woman who was to marry his uncle, King Mark. On the return voyage Tristan and Isolde swallowed a love potion by mistake. They fell in love and – although they then had to marry other people – they never stopped loving each other. When they died, King Mark had them buried side by side.

TROJAN WAR G: ten-year struggle between the citizens of Troy and an army of Greek invaders, caused by the capture of *Helen of Troy*, and described by *Homer* in the 'Iliad'. The leaders of the Greeks included Agamemnon, Ajax, *Achilles* and *Odysseus*. Unable to scale the walls of Troy, the Greeks sailed out of sight, leaving a huge wooden horse as an offering to *Athene*. The puzzled Trojans took it into their city, then at night – after the fleet returned – fifty champion Greek warriors emerged from the horse's belly and began the final massacre.

URANUS G: name given by the Greeks to the heavenly sky. In the beginning, Uranus joined with Ge, the Earth, to produce the race of *Titans*. One of these was Cronos (*Saturn*), who rose up and drove Uranus (the Sky) apart from Ge (the Earth) for ever.

VENUS R (Aphrodite G): goddess of love and beauty, ancestor of the Roman people. Although she herself was very beautiful, she was said to be married to the ugly god of craftsmen, Vulcan.

VIRGIL R: poet who wrote in the first century BC. His best-known but unfinished book, the 'Aeneid', tells an origin legend of the Roman nation, featuring the Trojan prince *Aeneas*.

VORTIGERN C: legendary king who ruled over Britain after the Romans left. When the Saxons invaded, he fled into Wales and tried to build a strong castle. But the foundations kept disappearing, and the boy *Merlin* explained that this was because a lake lay underneath, containing the sleeping red and white dragons buried by King Lludd (see *Fantastic creatures*). The dragons then began to fight again, the red one finally defeating the white. Merlin said that this showed that one day the red (Celtic) people would overcome the white (Saxon) invaders.

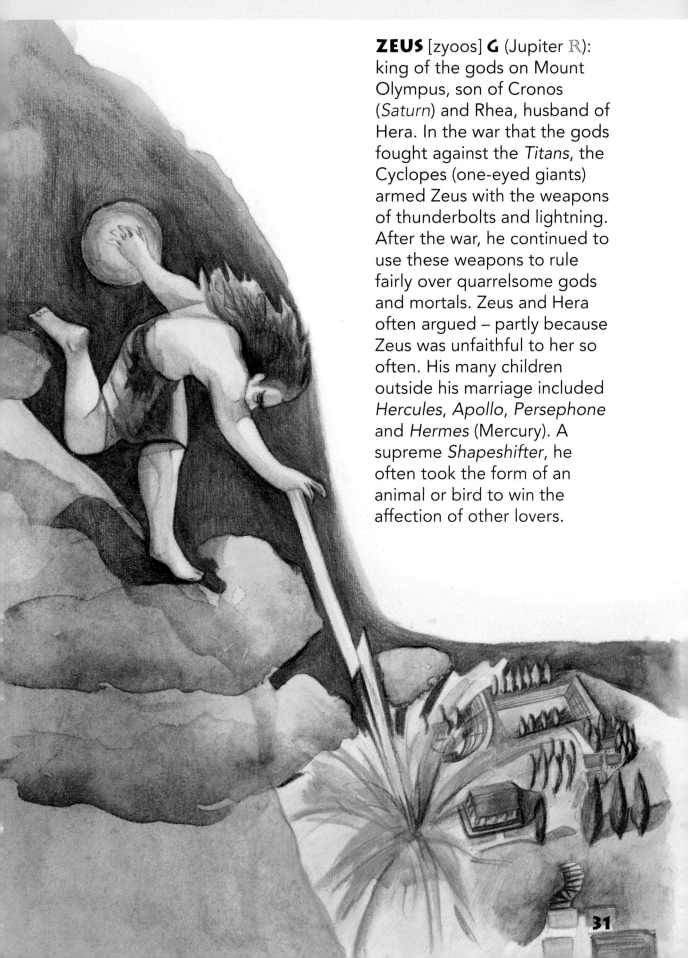

ZEUS [zyoos] **G** (Jupiter ℝ): king of the gods on Mount Olympus, son of Cronos (*Saturn*) and Rhea, husband of Hera. In the war that the gods fought against the *Titans*, the Cyclopes (one-eyed giants) armed Zeus with the weapons of thunderbolts and lightning. After the war, he continued to use these weapons to rule fairly over quarrelsome gods and mortals. Zeus and Hera often argued – partly because Zeus was unfaithful to her so often. His many children outside his marriage included *Hercules*, *Apollo*, *Persephone* and *Hermes* (Mercury). A supreme *Shapeshifter*, he often took the form of an animal or bird to win the affection of other lovers.

INDEX